Project Monster
ALPHABET ADVENTURE!

Written by:
Julie Robinson & Jay Santarossa

Illustrated by:
Julie Robinson

Copyright © 2020 by Project Monster Studios
ALL RIGHTS RESERVED.
This book or any portion thereof may not be reproduced or used in any manner whatsoever, without the expressed written permission of the publisher, except for the use of brief quotations in a book review. All Characters are created by Julie Robinson and are the property of Julie Robinson, and in no way shall they be used in any other publication or copied without the written permission of Julie Robinson.

Project Monster Studios
142 Santa Ana Ave.
Harrow, ON CANADA
N0R1G0

Independently Published
Second Edition, 2020
ISBN 9798677255403

www.projectmonster.ca
projectmonsterabc@gmail.com

A Special Thank You
to everyone who contributed to making this book a reality!!!

Janice & Dave Robinson, Sandy & Dave Santarossa,
Alfredo & Mary Santarossa, Carol & George Fenos,
Sarah-Jane Doiron Grant, Mike & Christa Realba,
Erin Deslippe, Kelly McWhinnie, Alexander McWilliam, Julie Roy,
Roderick Villaneuva, Chris D'Angelo, Suvi & Nico Colasanti, Kelly Fyke,
Anthony Mancini, Bonnie Deslippe, Scott & Bethany Fryer,
Christina Klein, Carl Chute, Mike & Cheryl Fox, Dana & Chris Barresi,
Nathan Bezaire, The Comb & Sammy Brush, Allison Beaudoin,
Gino Nicoletti, Bright Child Montessori, Yvonne Heerma,
Isabelle Archambault, Andi Trindle Mersch, Diana & Jeff Brady,
Barb Fryer, Pat McCaffery, Barb Hay, Katrina Peters,
Linda O'Brien Moldovan, John Tregaskiss, Nancy Lucier, Laura Giffin,
Jan Smith, Richard Deslippe, Sandy Kennedy, Kenny & Lindsay Skene

**Extra Special Thanks to
Nathalie Roy
for your professional advice
and inspiring ideas!**

Project Monster was eager, energetic and set,

To learn every letter, in the whole Alphabet!

"Oh! Hello Spirit Bear,
what do you say?"

"Let's take an adventure,
and learn the letters that way!"

"What a wonderful plan, but first we should pack,
Some important supplies, like a camera and snacks!"

"We can take a nice picture, of each of our friends,

To remember them all, from beginning to end!"

"There are 26 letters to learn and to read,

Let's find all our friends, from A down to Z."

First **Angus the Angler**, chased his light to the top,

"He can **Act As** our "**A**", lets get a good shot!"

"Look over there, see that Spirit Bear?"

"I'm excited no doubt, let's go check it out!"

Bunskis was **B**ashful,
Blushing and **B**rave,
She took a great picture,
and then **B**ounced away.

"Crabby McCrabberson, Can represent "C"!"
As the Camera snapped, Crabby said "Cheeese."

Dragon McFly,
was Dancing as "D",
While Ellie the Elephant,
was Everything "E"!

Friendly and **F**ast, they knew who was next, **F**roggy Mc**F**roggerson, was a **F**antastic "**F**"!

Then Spirit Bear heard,
a **G**reat **G**itty sound,

It was **Gary Giraffe**,
"What's he **G**iggling about?"

"**H**ammy the **H**amster,
Had a **H**ilarious joke",

"Thats "G" and thats "H"..."
Project Monster was stoked!

They all had a laugh, cause the joke was so funny,

Then Spirit Bear said, "I'm feeling so hungry!"

They walked up the hill, to take a short break,
Saw Illy Iguana, and Jam the Ram by the lake!

Project Monster took pictures, for "I" and for "J", Soon Kapow Kangaroo, was Keen to be "K".

"Look! Lulu Llama!" Spirit Bear could just tell, She was Lingering Lakeside, and would Love to be "L"!

Mack Mongoose Moved over,
Near Nutty the Squirrel,
Their Magnificent tails,
were Nestled and curled.

While Owelie Observed,
Overtop in the tree,
Pigskis Played by the Pond,
he was Perfectly "P".

Project Monster snapped pictures, of the whole Kung-Fu crew,

It was time to move on, to the next letter "Q".

Quickly they **R**an,
to the sound of the tunes,
It was **Q**uirky the **Q**uail
and **R**adio **R**accoon.

The **Q**uad **R**ock n' **R**olled,
with "**Q**" and with "**R**",
Then were off to find "**S**",
which couldn't be far.

Swimming and **S**plashing, **T**rading **T**ales in the **S**ea, **S**quidskis played ball, with his pal **T**urtley!

Spirit Bear **S**plashed, with "**S**" and with "**T**", A good pic was clicked, then what did they **S**ee?

They saw **U**ni the **U**nicorn,
Up by the cave,
She was **U**niquely "**U**",
and happy that way!

Von the Swan was as Vibrant, as Willow the Whale, Snap Went the camera, splash Went their tails!

Xavier C. Otter,
put his paws up and fleXed,
Project Monster said "Thanks,
you're such a great "X"."

Yawning a bit, Project Monster looked back, and that's when he saw, good ole' **Y**akidy **Y**ak!

Yapping over **Y**onder, talking all about "**Y**", **Y**akidy **Y**akked for a while, and then waved him goodbye.

Last but not least, was the **KING** of them **ALL**,
It was **Z**ion the **L**ion who stood proud and stood tall!

Zion was **Z**any!
They made it to "**Z**",
"Our adventure is over, let's go look and see!"

"You've done a great job, Project Monster and Friends, Now it's time to remember, all the letters again!"

27

A – **Angus**

B – **Bunskis**

C – **Crabby**

D – **Dragon**

E – **Ellie**

F - **Froggy**

G - **Gary**

H - **Hammy**

I - **Illy**

J - **Jam**

29

K - Kapow

L - Lulu

M - Mack **N - Nutty**

O - Owelie

P - Pigskis

Q - Quirky

R - Radio

S - Squidskis

T - Turtley

U - Uni

31

V - **V**on

W - **W**illow

X - **X**avier

Y - **Y**akidy

Z - **Z**ion

Made in the USA
Monee, IL
15 December 2021